The Great Adventures of
Pico the Chug

Lost and Found

Written by
Jessica A Schneider

Illustrations by
Mae Elizabeth Acuña

ISBN 978-1-66786-572-0

Dedicated to Pico, who was lost and then found.

In a really big town
on a cold winter day,
Pico is lost,
with nowhere to stay.

She finds a warm porch
and tucks herself in
for warmth and protection
from the bitter wind.

Twelve-year-old Cora
is just heading out,
when she opens the door
and gives a great shout:
"Oh my!" she exclaims.
"Are you lost in this storm?
It's so cold outside.
We must get you warm!"

Pico shakes! Pico shivers!

She gives a small cry.

Cora jumps into action and brings her inside.

Pico gets milk and some leftover stew

while Cora decides what more she can do.

Pico is small, a cute little chug.

One half Chihuahua, the other half Pug.

Her coat is the color of a fresh hay bale.

One ear up, one ear down, with a curlicue tail.

"There must be a family missing you, pooch."

"Don't worry," she says, "we'll find them for you!"

With help from her mom, Cora gets right to work.

She makes up a list of the places she'll search.

She snaps a quick pic
to make up some signs.
Do you know this pup?
If so, call this line!

She calls all her neighbors, the shelters, the pound.

But no one knows Pico, no owner's been found.

Days come and go, but no one responds,

while Pico and Cora continue to bond.

"Well girl," says Cora, "looks like you're alone."

"How would you like to stay here in our home?"

Pico is happy! No longer a stray!

She loves Cora's family and was hoping to stay.

With Cora at school, Pico's all on her own.

She wanders around by herself in their home.

With no proper toys, she finds a great shoe.

It's fuzzy and soft and perfect to chew!

The days are so long, at times she can't hold it.

She knows it's not right, but she pees on the carpet.

She nibbles her dinner,

but her new food tastes funny.

It rumbles and tumbles around in her tummy.

At bedtime she's put in a room with no light.

The darkness is scary

and she cries through the night.

Cora is frazzled by her new little pup.

Pico thinks sadly,

"Will she give me up?"

Cora's friend Johnny lives one house away.

He visits with Cora while his mom works all day.

Saturday morning brings a big surprise:

"A dog!" exclaims Johnny, finding Pico inside.

Pico greets Johnny with a sweet little yelp.

"Can we play?" he asks Cora,

and she's glad for the help.

Cora describes how she found the small pup.

They looked for an owner, but finally gave up.

"She seems to be lost, a true runaway.

I wanted a dog, and mom let her stay."

"It was great at the start,
but it's not what I thought."

"This week's been hard,
and she seems so distraught."

Johnny considers, and offers his view.

"If I was alone, I'd be scared too.

I'm on my own when my mom works all day,

but I have my toys, and friends come to play."

Cora hugs Johnny.

"Of course, now I see!

It's my job to take care of all Pico's needs!"

That night, Cora works on a plan for their home,
to make it more comfy when Pico's alone.

She finds lots of toys for Pico to chew.

Some fuzzy

 Some squeaky

Some
purple and blue.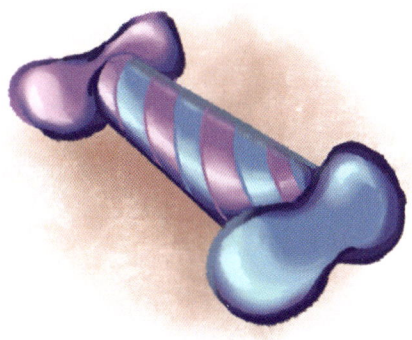

She sets up a nice cozy space for her bed,
with blankets and pillows and lights overhead.

Next on her list is a little bit hard.

She installs a dog door to the grassy backyard.

"It's worth it," she thinks, as she fits it in place.

"Now Pico can go in and out at her pace."

With help from her mom, she calls up the vet
to make an appointment for her little pet.

The doctor examines the chug, tail to lips,
while offering Cora a few pet-care tips.

Finally done, Cora's bursting with pride.

Pico is happy and beams by her side.

"Well Pico," says Cora, "Our first week was rough!"

"I didn't know owning a dog was so tough.

I made some mistakes, but I learned the right way

to care for your needs, day after day."

Pico is thrilled; she's found her new place.

She sits up and licks Cora right in the face!

Cora grabs Pico and gives her a hug.

It's time for adventures of Pico the Chug!

The End